MOTIVATIONAL QUOTES FOR COACHES, CAPTAINS AND TEAM LEADERS

Compilation and Commentary
By
Lawrence Newman

Motivational Quotes for Coaches, Captains and Team Leaders

Copyright © 2015 by Lawrence Newman

ISBN 978-0-9864201-4-6

Library of Congress Control Number: 2015901696

Printed in the United States of America

First Edition

Publisher: Silver Millennium Publications, Inc.
         South Elgin, Illinois
         www.silvermillpub.com

Other books by the author

365 Outstanding Quotes That Could Change Your Life

1000 Outstanding Quotes You Should Know

Treasury of "On Target" Humorous Quotes For Public Speakers

The Apostle Islands — America's Wilderness In The Water

Discovering The Apostle Islands

Sailing Adventures In The Apostle Islands

*Tales Of A Nautical Novice:
Lessons I Learned Boating In The Great Lakes*

Traveler's Guide To Wisconsin's Lake Superior Shore

The Eternal Question: Does God Exist?

Self-Publishing Your Book: A Nuts and Bolts Approach

MOTIVATIONAL QUOTES FOR COACHES, CAPTAINS AND TEAM LEADERS

"Sometimes doing your best isn't good enough. Sometimes you need to do what is required."—Winston Churchill

"I fear not the man who has practiced 10,000 kicks once, but I fear the man who has practiced one kick 10,000 times."—Bruce Lee

"Take risks and you'll get the payoffs. Learn from your mistakes until you succeed. It's that simple."—Bobby Flay

"Hope is not a strategy. Luck is not a factor. Fear is not an option."—James Cameron. This quote was on the shirts given to the staff members working on the motion picture *Avatar*.

"Winning isn't everything, but wanting to win is."—Vince Lombardi

"Nobody can go back and make a new beginning, but anyone can start a new ending."—Unknown

"The world steps aside for any man who knows where he's going."—Unknown

"Do you love life? Then do not squander time for that's the stuff life is made of."—Benjamin Franklin

"It's the little details that are vital. Little things make big things happen."—John Wooden

"Tomorrow, in a very real sense, your life—the life you author from scratch on your own—begins. . . I will hazard a prediction. When you are 80 years old, and in a quiet moment of reflection narrating for only yourself the most personal version of your life story, the telling that will be most compact and meaningful will be the series of choices you have made. In the end, *we are our choices. Build yourself a great story.*"—Jeff Bezos, Amazon.com CEO, from a commencement address at Princeton University, May 30, 2010.

"If you aim at nothing you will hit it every time."—Zig Ziglar

"I must not fear. Fear is the mind-killer. Fear is the little-death that brings total obliteration. I will face my fear."—Bene Gesseret

"As long as you live, keep learning how to live."—Seneca

"Do you want to know who you are? Don't ask. Act! Action will delineate and define you."—Thomas Jefferson

"Nobody makes a greater mistake than he who did nothing because he could only do a little."—Edmund Burke

"If you don't like your life, change it. You are the artist; you have the canvas, brushes, and colors."—Nikos Kazantzakis

"Here is a test to find whether your mission on earth is finished: If you're alive, it isn't."—Richard D. Bach

"Patience, persistence and perspiration make an unbeatable combination for success."—Napoleon Hill

"Remember that what you possess in this world will be found on the day of your death to belong to somebody else. But what you are will be yours forever."—Henry Van Dyke

"The greatest mistake you can make in life is to be continually fearing you will make one."—Elbert Hubbard

"You'd be surprised at how much you can accomplish if you don't care who gets the credit."—Ronald Reagan

"Continuous effort, not strength or intelligence, is the key to unlocking your potential."—Winston Churchill

"You can still take charge of your education, and of your lives. The cocoon years are over; the micro-aggressions are about to pour down. Deal with it. Revel in it. No consequential idea ever failed to offend someone; no consequential person was ever spared great offense. Those of you who want to lead meaningful lives need to begin unlearning, most of what you've been taught, starting right now."—Bret Stephens, in a commentary in *The Wall Street Journal,* castigating the attitude of college students about to graduate who take offense at anything, or anyone, who makes them feel uncomfortable.

"Twenty years from now you will be more disappointed by the things you didn't do than by the things you did do. So throw off the bow lines. Sail away from the safe harbor. Catch the trade winds in your sails. Explore. Dream Discover."—Mark Twain

"No one can cheat you out of ultimate success but yourself."—Ralph Waldo Emerson

"Know that life is not fair and that you will fail often, but if you take some risks, step up when the times are toughest, face down the bullies, lift up the downtrodden and never, ever give up—if you do these things, then next generation and the generations that follow will live in a world far better than the one we have today and—what started here will indeed have changed the world for the better."—Closing comments of a commencement speech to the 2014 graduating class of University of Texas by U. S. Navy Admiral William McRaven, commander of U. S. Special Operations Command, which includes the Navy Seals group that killed Osama bin Laden.

"Change is the law of life. And those who look only to the past or present are certain to miss the future."—President John F. Kennedy

"As to methods, there may be a million, and then some, but principles are few. The man who grasps principles can successfully select his own methods."—Ralph Waldo Emerson

"I expect to pass through life but once. If therefore, there be any kindness I can show, or any good thing I can do to any fellow being, let me do it now, and not defer or neglect it, as I shall not pass this way again."—William Penn

"Tomorrow is promised to no one."—Walter Payton

"You are no bigger than the things that annoy you."—Jerry Bundsen

"Life is 10% of what happens to you and 90% how you react to it."— Charles Swindell

"Without faith nothing is possible. With it nothing is impossible."—Unknown

"Anyone who stops learning is old, whether at twenty or eighty. Anyone who keeps learning is young. The greatest thing in life is to keep your mind young."—Henry Ford

"Just say 'no'."—Antidrug slogan associated with Nancy Reagan

"If you don't care where you end up in life, you can take any road to get there."—Unknown

"You have to have a vision. It's got to be a vision you articulate clearly and forcefully. You can't blow an uncertain trumpet."—Rev. Theodore Hesburgh, Notre Dame University

"Once you say you're going to settle for second, that's what happens to you in life, I find."—President John F. Kennedy

"Nothing in the world can take the place of persistence. Talent will not; nothing is more common than unsuccessful men of talent. Genius will not; unrewarded genius is almost a proverb. Education will not; the world is full of educated derelicts. Persistence and determination alone are omnipotent."—President Calvin Coolidge

"O God, give us serenity to accept what cannot be changed, courage to change what should be changed, and wisdom to distinguish the one from the other."—Reinhard Niebur (The Serenity Prayer)

"If you fail to plan, you plan to fail."—Unknown

"Leadership is the act of getting someone else to do something you want done because he wants to do it."—President Dwight Eisenhower

"He has half the deed done who has made a beginning."—Horace

"The pessimist sees the difficulty in every opportunity. The optimist sees the opportunity in every difficulty."—Winston Churchill

"The harder you work, the luckier you get."—Gary Player, professional golfer

"Better to go forward with an imperfect plan pursued with vigor at the earliest opportunity, than a perfect plan too late."—General George Patton

"Those who stand for nothing fall for anything."—Alexander Hamilton

"Success isn't permanent, and failure isn't fatal."—Mike Ditka

"Never tell people how to do things. Tell them what to do and they will surprise you with their ingenuity."—General George Patton

"The ability to rest the mind and the power of dismissing from it all care and worry is probably one of the secrets of great men."—Captain J. A. Hatfield.

"He who laughs, lasts."—Mary Pettibone Poole

"The best place to start looking when we are having problems in dealing with others is the last place we look—the mirror."—Unknown

"I love the challenge of starting at zero every day and seeing how much I can accomplish."—Martha Stewart

"Anxiety is caused by lack of control, organization, preparation and action." —David Kekich

"Do not let what you cannot do interfere with what you can do."—John Wooden

"The secret of getting ahead is getting started. The secret of getting started is breaking your complex overwhelming tasks into small manageable tasks and starting on the first one."—Mark Twain

"The important thing is to learn a lesson every time you lose."—John McEnroe

"You always pass failure on the way to success."—Mickey Rooney

"Use wisely your power of choice."—Og Mandino

"You ain't learning when you're talking."—President Lyndon Johnson

"Planning for the future without a sense of the past is like planting cut flowers."—Daniel Boorstin, Pulitzer Prize winning historian

"We don't receive wisdom; we must discover it for ourselves after a journey that no one can take for us or spare us."—Marcel Proust

"Failure is instructive. The person who really thinks learns quite as much from his failures as his successes."—John Dewey

"A liar needs a good memory."—Quintilian

"No man has a memory long enough to be a successful liar."—Abraham Lincoln

"Fortune favors the bold."—Virgil

"We are the choices we make"—Meryl Streep

"Remember that a man's name is to him the sweetest and most important sound in the language."—Dale Carnegie, author of *How to Win Friends and Influence People*.

"Belief in God and in immortality gives us the moral strength and the ethical guidance we need for virtually every action in our daily lives."—Rocket scientist Wernher von Braun

"It is better to light one candle than to curse the darkness."—Motto of the Christopher Society

"Sandwich every bit of criticism between two thick layers of praise."—Mary Kay Ash

"If you rest, you rust"—Helen Hayes

"The greatest remedy for anger is delay."—Seneca

"You miss 100% of the shots you don't take."—Wayne Gretzky

"Don't make the mistake of letting yesterday use up too much of today."—Will Rogers

"When you're through changing, you're through."—Bruce Barton

"Speak when you are angry and you will make the best speech you will ever regret."—Ambrose Bierce

"Moderation in everything."–Aristotle

"I have missed more than 9000 shots in my career. I have lost almost 300 games. On 26 occasions I have been entrusted to take the game's winning shot...and missed. And I have failed over and over and over again in my life. And that is why...I succeed."—Michael Jordan

"Expect trouble as an inevitable part of life and repeat to yourself the most comforting words of all: This, too, shall pass."—Ann Landers

"The golden rule of life is, make a beginning."—American proverb

"Surround yourself with the best people you can find, delegate authority, and don't interfere."—President Ronald Reagan, describing his philosophy regarding his staff and cabinet.

"This thing we call failure is not the falling down, but the staying down."—Mary Pickford

"Our lives begin to end the day we become silent about things that matter."—Rev Martin Luther King, Jr.

"Be the change you wish to see in the world."—Mahatma Gandhi

"In life, as in a football game, the principle to follow is: Hit the line hard."—Theodore Roosevelt

"The individual's self-concept is the core of his personality. It affects every aspect of human behavior--the ability to learn, the capacity to grow and change. A strong, positive self-image is the best possible preparation for success in life."—Dr. Joyce Brothers

"In times of great stress or adversity, it's always best to keep busy, to plow your anger and your energy into something positive."—Lee Iacocca

"The way I see it, if you want the rainbow you gotta put up with the rain."—Dolly Parton

"The best way to predict your future is to create it."—Peter Drucker

"Courage is doing what you're afraid to do. There is no courage unless you're scared."—Eddie Richenbacker

"Without discipline there's no life at all."—Katherine Hepburn

"It's not fair to ask of others what you are unwilling to do yourself."—Eleanor Roosevelt

"Lack of something to feel important about is almost the greatest tragedy a man can have."—Arthur Morgan

"Individual commitment to a group effort—that is what makes a team work, a company work, a civilization work."—Coach Vince Lombardi

"Great moments are born from great opportunities."—Coach Herb Brooks, to members of the gold medal winning 1980 U. S. Olympic hockey team prior to their game with the Russians, who were heavily favored to win the match.

"With each choice you make, you create your life."—Unknown

"Character is doing what's right when nobody is looking."—Congressional Representative J. C. Watts, Jr.

"You can tell more about a person by what he says about others than you can by what others say about him."—Leo Aikman

"I didn't waste time."—Bill Gates, Microsoft founder, in response to a question as to the most important factor leading to his success.

"Nothing is more destined to create deep-seated anxieties in people than the false assumption that life should be free from anxieties."—Archbishop Fulton Sheen

"If you wouldn't write it and sign it, don't say it."—Earl Wilson

"I make progress by having people around who are smarter than I am, and listening to them."—Henry J. Kaiser

"We cannot change the cards we are dealt, just how we play the hand."—Randy Pausch, from "The Last Lecture".

"To know the road ahead, ask those coming back."—Chinese proverb

"You're only as good as the people you hire."—Ray Kroc, president of McDonald's

"Time is really the only capital that any human being has, and the only thing he can't afford to lose."—Thomas Edison

"Even if you're on the right track, you'll get run over if you just sit there."—Will Rogers

"Giving up is the ultimate tragedy."—Robert J. Donovan

"When I stand before God at the end of my life, I would hope that I would not have a single bit of talent left, and could say, 'I used everything you gave me'."—Erma Bombeck

"Promise only what you can deliver. Then deliver more than you promise."—Unknown

"Take time to deliberate, but when the time for action arrives, stop thinking and go in."—President Andrew Jackson

"Nothing strengthens the judgment and quickens the conscience like individual responsibility."—Elizabeth Cady Stanton

"You can make more friends in a month by being interested in them than in ten years by trying to get them interested in you."—Charles L. Allen

"Luck is what happens when preparation meets opportunity."—Seneca

"Most problems precisely defined are already partially solved."—Harry Lorayne

"Tell me who you're with and I'll tell you who you are."—Spanish proverb

"What have you done today to help reach your lifelong goals?"—Brian Tracy

"Our lives improve only when we take chances—and the first and most difficult risk we can take is to be honest with ourselves."—Walter Anderson

"There are times when silence has the loudest voice."—Leroy Brownlow

"By recording your dreams and goals on paper, you set in motion the process of becoming the person you most want to be."—Mark Victor Hansen

"Courage is contagious. When a brave man takes a stand, the spines of others are stiffened."—Rev. Billy Graham

"There are no secrets to success. It is the result of preparation, hard work, learning from failure."—General Colin Powell

"Never stop learning. If you learn one new thing every day, you will overcome 99% of your competition."—Joe Carlozo

"Whoever said, 'It's not whether you win or lose that counts,' probably lost."—Martina Navritilova

"Never give in—never... never... never."—Sir Winston Churchill, in a commencement address he gave at Harrow, the prep school he attended as a young boy.

"Those who are blessed with the most talent don't necessarily outperform everyone else. It's the people with follow-through who excel."—Mary Kay Ash

"When you have to make a choice and don't make it, that is in itself a choice."—William James

"The more arguments you win, the fewer friends you will have."—American proverb

"There is no comparison between that which is lost by not succeeding and that which is lost by not trying."—Francis Bacon

"There are no shortcuts to any place worth going."—Beverly Sills

"Decision is a sharp knife that cuts clean and straight. Indecision is a dull one that hacks and tears and leaves jagged edges behind."—Jan McKeithen

"Between tomorrow's dream and   yesterday's regret   is today's opportunity."—Unknown

"Trust yourself. You know more than you think you do."—Dr. Benjamin Spock

"The   obvious   choice   is usually a quick regret."—American proverb

"Excuses are the nails to build a house of failure."—Don Wilder

"We make a living by what we get, but we make a life by what we give."—Sir Winston Churchill

"The person who knows how will always have a job. But the person who knows why will be his boss."—Carl C. Wood

"When the going gets tough, the tough get going."—Unknown. Motto seen printed, in large letters, on the barracks wall of the Heavy Weapons Platoon of Company B, 1st Airborne Battle Group, 503rd Infantry, 82nd Airborne Division, Fort Bragg, North Carolina, in February 1959.

"If you see no reason to give thanks, the fault lies in yourself."—Native American proverb

"Cause change and lead; accept change and survive; resist change and die."—Ray Norda

"No one can make you feel inferior without your consent."—Eleanor Roosevelt

"I am the captain of my soul. I am the master of my fate."—William Henley, from his poem *Invictus*.

"If your actions inspire others to dream more, learn more, and become more, you are a leader."—John Quincy Adams

"People who are afraid to fail can never experience the joys of success."—Unknown

"The most prominent place in hell is reserved for those who are neutral on the great issues of life."—Rev. Billy Graham

"If you risk nothing, then you risk everything."—Geena Davis

"Don't be afraid to take a big step if one is indicated. You can't cross a chasm in two small jumps."—David Lloyd George

"When one door closes, another opens; but we often look so long and so regretfully upon the closed door that we do not see the one which has opened to us."—Alexander Graham Bell

"He who asks a question may be a fool for five minutes; he who never asks a question remains a fool forever."—Unknown

"The pessimist complains about the wind; the optimist expects it to change; the realist adjusts the sails."—William Arthur Ward

"Most people spend more time and energy going around problems than trying to solve them."—Henry Ford

"If you find a path with no obstacles, it probably doesn't lead anywhere."—Frank A. Clark

"Inaction breeds doubt and fear. Action breeds confidence and courage. If you want to conquer fear, do not sit home and think about it. Go out and get busy."—Dale Carnegie

"The trouble with not having a goal is that you can spend your life running up and down the field and never scoring."—Bill Copeland

"If you have an important point to make, don't try to be subtle or clever. Use a pile driver. Hit the point once. Then come back and hit it again. Then hit it a third time a tremendous whack."—Winston Churchill

"If you would thoroughly know anything, teach it to others."—Tryon Edwards

"Find something to laugh about."—Maya Angelou

"The art of being happy lies in the power of extracting happiness from common things."—Henry Ward Beecher

"Our greatest glory is not in never falling, but in rising every time we fall.—Confucius

"There's no such thing as work-life balance. There are work-life choices, and you make them and they have consequences."—Jack Welch, CEO, General Electric

"A hundred times a day I remind myself that my inner and outer life depends on the labors of other men, living and dead, and that I must exert myself in order to give in the same measure as I have received and am still receiving."—Albert Einstein

"The most important thing in communication is to hear what isn't being said."—Peter Drucker.

"The greatest danger for most men lies not in setting our aim too high and falling short, but in setting our aim too low and achieving our mark."—Michelangelo

"You can't steal second base and keep one foot on first."—Frederick B. Wilson

"Live your dreams one step at a time."— Inscription written on a World MS flag held by Lori Schneider, resident of Bayfield, Wisconsin, and afflicted with multiple sclerosis, during a photo taken on top of Mount Everest in July 2009. Lori, the first person with multiple sclerosis to climb Mount Everest, presented the flag to the Multiple Sclerosis Inter-national offices in London as an inspiration to all those suffering from the disease.

"God gives every bird his worm but He does not throw it into the nest."—Swedish proverb

"In three words I can sum up everything I've learned about life: It goes on."—Robert Frost

"You can conquer almost any fear if you will only make up your mind to do it. For remember, it doesn't exist anywhere but in the mind."—Dale Carnegie

"Everyone has an invisible sign hanging from their neck saying, 'Make me feel important'. Never forget this message when working with people."—Mary Kay Ash

"The art of leadership is saying no, not yes. It is very easy to say yes."—Tony Blair

"The only inexcusable offense in a commanding officer is to be surprised."—Motto pinned on the wall behind the desk of General Matthew B. Ridgway.

"Remember, gentlemen, an order that can be misunderstood will be misunderstood." —General von Moltke, Prussian general

"A handful of common sense is worth a bushel of learning."—Unknown

"Fired by success—they could do it because they believed they could do it."—Virgil

"To avoid criticism, do nothing, say nothing, be nothing."—Elbert Hubbard

"If I have lost confidence in myself, I have the Universe against me."—Ralph Waldo Emerson

"He who would learn to command well must first of all learn to obey."—Greek saying

"Today is the first day of the rest of your life."—Charles Dederich

"If there is one single secret to long life, that secret is moderation."—George Gallup

"In playing ball, and in life, a person occasionally gets the opportunity to do something great. When that time comes, only two things matter: being prepared to seize the moment and having the courage to take your best swing."—Hank Aaron

"Never, never waste a minute on regret. It's a waste of time."—Harry S. Truman

"Don't compare your life to others. You have no idea what their journey is all about"—Regina Britt

"All truly wise thoughts have been thought already thousands of times; but to make them truly ours, we must think them over again honestly, till they take root in our personal experience."—Goethe

"Speak the truth, but speak it palatably."—Sanscrit proverb

"What may be done at any time will be done at no time."—Scottish proverb

"Keep your fears to yourself; share your courage with others."—Robert Louis Stevenson

"Life isn't fair but it's still good."—Regina Britt

"Let me tell you the secret that has led me to my goal.   My secret lies solely in my tenacity."—Louis Pasteur

"Show me a thoroughly satisfied man and I will show you a failure."—Thomas Edison

"As soon as you trust yourself, you will know how to live."—Goethe

"There are only two ways to live your life. One is as though nothing is a miracle. The other is as though everything is a miracle."—Albert Einstein

"Pick battles big enough to matter, small enough to win."—Jonathan Kozel

"The future belongs to people who see possibilities before they become obvious."—Ted Levitt

"Be not inhospitable to strangers—Lest they be angels in disguise."—Yeats

"I can feel guilty about the past, apprehensive about the future, but only in the present can I act. The ability to be in the present moment is a major component of mental wellness."—Abraham Maslow

"No problem can withstand the assault of sustained thinking."—Voltaire

"If your project doesn't work, look for the part that you didn't think was important."—Arthur Bloch

"One way to get high blood pressure is to go mountain climbing over molehills."—Earl Wilson

"God gave you a gift of 86,400 seconds today. Have you used one to say 'thank you'."—William A. Ward

"We aim above the mark to hit the mark."—Ralph Waldo Emerson

"You don't get to choose how you're going to die. Or when. You *can* decide how you're going to live *now*."—Joan Baez

"In life, all good things come hard, but wisdom is the hardest to come by."—Lucille Ball

"Whatever you think it's gonna take, double it. That applies to money, time, stress. It's gonna be harder than you think and take longer than you think."—Richard Cortese, on starting your own business. These words are just as applicable to any large project.

"Nothing great was ever achieved without enthusiasm."—Ralph Waldo Emerson

"Silent gratitude isn't very much to anyone."—Gertrude Stein

"One man with courage is a majority."—Thomas Jefferson

"There are three kinds of people; those that make things happen, those that watch things happen and those who don't know what's happening."—American proverb

"Give yourself something to work toward—constantly."—Mary Kay Ash

"Efficiency is doing things right; effectiveness is doing the right things."—Peter Drucker

"Do the thing you fear to do and keep on doing it... that is the quickest and surest way ever yet discovered to conquer fear."—Dale Carnegie.

"Feeling sorry for yourself, and your present condition, is not only a waste of energy but the worst habit you could possibly have."—Dale Carnegie

"Make yourself necessary to somebody."—Ralph Waldo Emerson

Our life is frittered away by detail... simplify, simplify."—Henry David Thoreau

"Go confidently in the direction of your dreams. Live the life you have imagined."—Henry David Thoreau

"There are four ways, and only four ways, in which we have contact with the world. We are evaluated and classified by these four contacts: what we do, how we look, what we say, and how we say it."—Dale Carnegie

"Talent alone won't make you a success. Neither will being in the right place at the right time, unless you are ready. The most important question is: 'Are you ready?'"—Johnny Carson

"Plans are only good intentions unless they immediately degenerate into hard work."—Peter Drucker

"Opportunities are usually disguised as hard work, so most people don't recognize them."—Ann Landers

"Every man builds his world in his own image. He has the power to choose, but no power to escape the necessity of choice."—Ayn Rand

"If you're alive, there's a purpose for your life. You were made by God and for God, and until you understand that, life will never make sense."—Rick Warren, church founder and author of "A Purpose Driven Life".

"Death is a challenge. It tells us not to waste time... It tells us to tell each other right now that we love each other."—Leo Buscaglia

"All endeavor calls for the ability to tramp the last mile, shape the last plan, endure the last hour's toil. The fight to the finish spirit is the one characteristic we must possess if we are to face the future as finishers."—Henry David Thoreau

"If your head tells you one thing, and your heart tells you another, before you do anything, you should first decide whether you have a better head or a better heart."—Marilyn vos Savant

"Today is life—the only life you are sure of. Make the most of today. Get interested in something. Shake yourself awake. Let the winds of enthusiasm sweep through you. Live today with gusto."—Dale Carnegie

"The best way out is always through."—Robert Frost

"Be able to defend your arguments in a rational way. Otherwise, all you have is an opinion."—Marilyn vos Savant

"When you reach the end of your rope, tie a knot in it and hang on."—Thomas Jefferson

"There are two things people want more than sex and money... recognition and praise."—Mary Kay Ash

"You can have everything in life you want, if you will just help other people get what they want."—Zig Ziglar

"There is no such thing as a minor lapse of integrity."—Tom Peters

"Too often we underestimate the power of a touch, a smile, a kind word, a listening ear, an honest compliment, or the smallest act of caring, all of which have the potential to turn a life around."—Leo Buscaglia

"What you get by achieving your goals is to as important as what you become by achieving your goals."—Henry David Thoreau

"The line between failure and success is so fine that we scarcely know when we pass it: so fine that we are often on the line and do not know it."—Elbert Hubbard

"Nobody gets to live life backward. Look ahead. That is where your future lies."—Ann Landers

"This is all you have. This is not a dry run. This is your life. If you want to fritter it away with your fears, then you will fritter it away, but you won't get it back later."—Laura Schlessinger

"Lead, follow, or get out of the way."—Thomas Paine

"It's surprising how many persons go through life without ever recognizing that their feelings toward other people are largely determined by their feelings toward themselves, and if you're not comfortable within yourself, you can't be comfortable with others."—Sydney J. Harris

"A man who dares to waste one hour of time has not discovered the value of life."—Charles Darwin

"We must have a theme, a goal, a purpose in our lives. If you don't know where you're aiming, you don't have a goal. My goal is to live my life in such a way that when I die, someone can say, she cared."—Mary Kay Ash

"Listening, not imitation, may be the sincerest form of flattery."—Joyce Brothers

"Reduce your plan to writing. The moment you complete this, you will have definitively given concrete form to the intangible desire."—Napoleon Hill

"The greatest mistake you can make in life is continually fearing that you'll make one."— Elbert Hubbard

"I tell you the past is a bucket of ashes, so live not in your yesterdays."—Carl Sandburg

"The three hardest tasks in the world are neither physical feats nor intellectual achievements, but moral acts: to return love for hate, to include the excluded, and to say, 'I was wrong'."—Sydney J. Harris

"If you must speak ill of another, do not speak it, write it in the sand near the water's edge."— Napoleon Hill

"Time is the coin of your life. It is the only coin you have, and only you can determine how it will be spent. Be careful lest you let other people spend it for you."—Carl Sandburg

"I like to listen. I have learned a great deal from listening carefully. Most people never listen."—Ernest Hemingway

"Patience, persistence and perspiration make an unbeatable combination for success."—Napoleon Hill

"Wherever you go, go with all your heart."—Confucius

"Most people give up just when they're about to achieve success. They quit on the one-yard line. They give up at the last minute of the game one foot from a winning touchdown."—Ross Perot

"The most important single ingredient in the formula of success is knowing how to get along with people."—Theodore Roosevelt

"It's better to fight for something than against something."—Unknown

"Never be bullied into silence. Never allow yourself to be made a victim. Accept no one's definition of your life; define yourself."—Harvey Feirstein

"Your future depends on many things, but mostly on you."—Frank Tyger

"Do what you can, with what you have, where you are."—Theodore Roosevelt

"There are two types of people— those who come into a room and say, 'Well, here I am!' and those who come in and say, 'Ah, there you are!'"—Frederick L. Collins

"Don't go around saying the world owes you a living. The world owes you nothing. It was here first."—Mark Twain

"I can live for two months on a good compliment."—Mark Twain

"Half the failures of this world arise from pulling in one's horse as he is leaping."—Julius Hare

"The pursuit of the difficult makes men strong."—George Romney

"You were born to win, but to be a winner, you must plan to win, prepare to win, and expect to win."—Zig Ziglar

"Courage is not the lack of fear. It is acting in spite of it.—Unknown

"I'm a little wounded, but I am not slain/I will lay me down to bleed a while/Then I'll rise and fight again."—John Dryden

"Many people will walk in and out of your life but only true friends will leave footprints in your heart."—Unknown

"Constant and determined effort breaks down all resistance and sweeps away all obstacles."—Unknown

"It isn't that you can't see the solution. It is that you can't see the problem."—G. K. Chesterton

"With every rising of the sun, think of your life as just begun."—Unknown

"Optimism and pessimism are infectious and they spread more rapidly from the head downward than in any direction. With this clear realization I firmly determined that my mannerisms and speech in public would always reflect the cheerful certainty of victory—that any pessimism and discouragement I might ever feel would be reserved for my pillow."—General Dwight Eisenhower

"You are, of course, entitled to your own opinion—but you are not entitled to your own facts."—Unknown

"I hear and I forget. I see and I remember. I do and I understand."—Chinese proverb

"To say my fate is not tied to your fate is like saying 'Your end of the boat is sinking'."—Hugh Downs

"There are risks and costs to a program of action. But they are far less than the long-range risks and costs of comfortable inaction."—President John F. Kennedy

"If everybody is thinking alike then somebody isn't thinking."—General George Patton

"I do the very best I know how—the very best I can; and I mean to keep doing so until the end. If the end brings me out all right, what is said about me won't amount to anything. If the end brings me out wrong, ten angels swearing I was right would make no difference."—President Abraham Lincoln

"I went to the woods because I wished to live deliberately, to front only the essential facts of life, and see if I could not learn what it had to teach, and not, when I came to die, discover that I had not lived."—Henry Thoreau

"The conservative who resists change is as valuable as the radical who proposes it."—Will and Ariel Durant

"Only your real friends will tell you when your face is dirty."—Sicilian Proverb

"Give a man a fish and you feed him for a day. Teach him to fish and you feed him for a lifetime."—Chinese proverb

"Make no little plans; they have no magic to stir men's blood."—Chicago architect Daniel Burnham, describing his underlying philosophy for the planning of the 1893 World's Fair.

"You have enemies? Good. That means you've stood up for something, sometime in your life."—Winston Churchill

"Most of us have far more courage than we ever dreamed we possessed."—Dale Carnegie

"Need breaks iron."—Unknown

"Leadership is the capacity to translate vision into reality."—Warren G. Bennis

"Self respect is the root of discipline. The sense of dignity grows with the ability to say no to oneself."—Abraham Heschel

"Yes, I have doubted. I have wandered off the path, but I always return. It is intuitive, an intrinsic, built-in sense of direction. I seem always to find my way home. My faith has wavered but saved me."—Helen Hayes

"Security is mostly a superstition. It does not exist in nature, nor do the children of men as a whole experience it. Avoiding danger is no safer in the long run than outright exposure. Life is either a daring adventure or nothing."—Helen Keller

"The truth of the matter is you always know the right thing to do. The hard part is doing it."—General H. Norman Schwarzkopf

"The woods are lovely, dark and deep. But I have promises to keep. And miles to go before I sleep. And miles to go before I sleep."—Robert Frost, from his poem *Stopping by Woods on a Snowy Evening*.

"Don't complain. The people who will listen can't do anything about it, while the people who can do something about it won't listen."—John Hebert

"Figuring out who you are is the whole point of human experience."—Anna Quindlen

"The most difficult thing in the world is to know how to do something and to watch someone else doing it wrong without comment."—Theodore White

"If it's working, keep doing it. If it's not working, stop doing it. If you don't know what to do, don't do anything."—Medical School advice to prospective doctors.

"We know the truth, not only by reason, but also by the heart."—Blaise Pascal

"He who walks in the middle of the road gets hit from both sides."—George Schultz

"Each choice we make opens the door to other choices—and for better or for worse, our lives are the sum total of our decisions."—John Gardner

"Every day in every way I am getting better and better."—Unknown. But only if you make the effort.

"Two roads diverged in a wood, and I—,
I took the one less traveled by,
And that made all the difference."—From the
poem *The Road Less Traveled* by Robert Frost.

"Until the day of his death no man can be sure
of his courage."—Jean Anouilh

"Life is a grindstone; whether it grinds you
down or polishes you up depends on what
you're made of."—Jacob Braude

"Worry is like a rocking chair, it will give you
something to do, but it won't get you
anywhere."—Unknown

"Inspiration is contagious. Once inspired
you're capable of anything."—Unknown

"Great deeds are not done by strength or speed or physique. They are the products of thought, and character, and judgment."—Cicero

"Warmth is a communicable disease. If you haven't got it, no one will be able to catch it from you."—Robert Bass

"If I had to sum up in one word what makes a good manager, I'd say decisiveness."—Lee Iacocca

"Don't cry because it's over, smile because it happened."—Unknown

"The hardest thing to learn in life is which bridge to cross and which to burn."—David Russell

"Life is an echo. What you send out—you get back. What you give—you get."—Unknown

"Once a decision was made I did not worry about it afterward."—Harry Truman

"Success is peace of mind, which is a direct result of self-satisfaction in knowing you made the effort to do the best of which you are capable."—John Wooden

"When written in Chinese, the word 'crisis' is composed of two chararacters. One represents danger and the other represents opportunity."—John F. Kennedy

"You are never too old to be what you might have been."—George Eliot

"A goal without a plan is just a wish."—Antonine de Saint-Exupery

"There are two kinds of failure: those who thought and never did, and those who did but never thought." —Lawrence Peter

"The best and safest thing is to keep a balance in your life, acknowledge the great powers around us and in us. If you can do that, and live that way, you are really wise."—Euripides

"Don't judge each day by the harvest you reap, but by the seeds you plant."—Robert Louis Stevenson

"A creative man is motivated by the desire to achieve, not by the desire to beat others."—Ayn Rand

"Too much experience with winning tends to make us stupid (or at least lures us into a dangerous complacency). Winning makes you think you'll always get the girl, land the job, deposit the million-dollar check, win the promotion, and you grow accustomed to a life of answered prayers."—Pat Conroy. Sometimes losing makes us a better person in the long run and adjusts our perception of reality.

"Your big opportunity may be right where you are now."—Napoleon Hill

"The man who can drive himself further when the effort gets painful is the man who will win."—Roger Bannister, the first runner to break the four minute mile.

"Loneliness is the penalty of leadership."—Ernest Shackleton, leader of an historic exploration group to the Antarctic.

"Followers who tell the truth and leaders who listen are an unbeatable combination."—Warren Bennis

"A ship in harbor is safe, but that's not what ships are built for."—John Shedd. In other words, when warranted, take risks in your life.

"If you're not making mistakes, you're not trying hard enough."—Vince Lombardi

"The person who makes a success of living is the one who sees his goal steadily and aims for it unswervingly."—Cecil B. DeMille

"The successful warrior is the average man with laser-like focus."—Bruce Lee

"Build momentum by accumulating small successes."—Unknown

"There is no education like adversity."—Benjamin Disraeli

"Leadership is solving problems. The day soldiers stop bringing you their problems is the day you have stopped leading them. They have either lost confidence that you can help or concluded that you do not care. Either case is a failure of leadership."—General Colin Powell

"The indispensable first step to getting the things you want out of life is this: Decide what you want."—Ben Stein

"When you are in a contest, you should work as if there were, to the very last minute—a chance to lose it. This is battle, this is politics, this is anything."—Dwight D. Eisenhower

"Love him who tells you your faults in private."—Hebrew proverb

"If you treat every situation in life as a life-and-death matter, you'll die a lot of times."—Dean Smith

"A hunch is creativity trying to tell you something."—Frank Capra

"Admonish your friends privately, but praise them publicly."—Publius Syrus

"Next to knowing when to seize an opportunity, the most important thing in life is to know when to forego an advantage."—Benjamin Disrael

"Good losers get into the habit of losing."—George Allen

"People living deeply have no fear of death."—
Anais Nin

"Keep away from people who try to belittle
your ambitions. Small people always do that,
but the really great make you feel that you, too,
can become great."—Mark Twain

"Success cannot be guaranteed. There are no
safe battles."—Winston Churchill

"Nobody who tries to do something great but
fails is a total failure. He can always rest
assured that he succeeded in life's most
important battle—he defeated the fear of
trying."—Robert Schuller

"Dost thou love life? Then do not squander
time; for that's the stuff life is made of."—
Benjamin Franklin

"I don't want to get to the end of my life and find that I lived just the length of it. I want to have lived the width of it as well."—Diane Ackerman

"Once the facts are clear, the decisions jump out at you."—Peter Drucker

"In the fields of observation, chance favors only the prepared mind."—Louis Pasteur

"Once you get people laughing, they're listening and you can tell them almost anything."—Herbert Gardner

"Few things help an individual more than to place responsibility on him and let him know that you trust him."—Booker T. Washington

"A major reason capable people fail to advance is that they don't work well with their colleagues."—Lee Iaccoca

"One half the troubles of this life can be traced to saying 'yes' too often and not saying 'no' soon enough."—Josh Billings

"If anything goes bad, I did it. If anything goes semi-good, then we did it. If anything goes good, then you did it. That's all it takes to have people win football games for you."—Bear Bryant

"Nothing is particularly hard if you divide it into small jobs."—Henry Ford

"You can easily judge the character of a man by how he treats those who can do nothing for him."—James Miles

"(My father) used to say: Gather all the facts possible and then make your decision on what you think is right . . . Don't try to guess what others will think, whether they will praise or deride you. And always remember that at least some of your decisions will be wrong. Do this and you will always sleep well at night."— General Douglas MacArthur

"Men may doubt what you say but they will believe what you do."—Lewis Cass

"First-rate men hire first-rate men. Second-rate men hire third-rate men."—Leo Rosten

"You do not lead by hitting people over the head. That's assault, not leadership."—Dwight D. Eisenhower

"Life is a great canvas and you should throw all the paint on it you can."—Danny Kaye

"Each choice we make opens the door to other choices—and for better or for worse our lives are the sum total of our decisions."—John Gardner

"The leaders who offer blood, toil, tears and sweat always get more out of their followers than those who offer safety and a good time."—George Orwell

"Success covers a multitude of failures."—George Bernard Shaw

"Determine that the thing can and shall be done and we shall find the way."—Abraham Lincoln

"A life that hasn't a definite plan is likely to become driftwood."—David Sarnoff

"Change your life today. Don't gamble on the future, act now, without delay."—Simone de Beauvoir

"Someday I hope to enjoy enough of what the world calls success so that somebody will ask me, 'What's the secret of it?' I will say simply this: 'I get up when I fall down."—Paul Harvey

"Talk to a man about himself and he will listen for hours."—Benjamin Disraeli

"The days come and go like veiled and muffled figures sent from a distant friendly party, but they say nothing, and if we do not use the gifts they bring, they carry them as silently away."— Ralph Waldo Emerson

"The bitterest tears shed over graves are for words left unsaid and deeds left undone."— Harriet Beecher Stowe

"The difference between failure and success is doing a thing nearly right and doing a thing exactly right."—Edward Simmons

"Use what talents you possess: the woods would be very silent if no birds sang there except those who sang best."—Henry Van Dyke

"I was successful because you believed in me."—General Ulysses S. Grant to President Abraham Lincoln

"Always do what you say you're going to do. It is the glue and fiber that binds successful relationships."—Jeffry Timmons

"Besides the noble art of getting things done, there is the noble art of leaving things undone. The wisdom of life consists in the elimination of non-essentials."—Lin Yutang

"If you keep doing what you're doing you'll keep getting what you got."—Unknown

"I have always been delighted at the prospect of a new day, a fresh try, one more start, with perhaps a bit of magic waiting somewhere behind the morning."—J. B. Priestly

"Probably the most honest 'self-made' man ever was the one we heard say, 'I got to the top the hard way—fighting my own laziness and ignorance every step of the way'."—James Thom

"When you're up against a tough problem, never quit. There's always one more thing you can do to influence any situation in your favor. And then after that, one more thing again. Never give up."—Retired Lt. Gen. Hal Moore, 40 years after leading his battalion to victory during a savage battle in the Ia Drang Valley in Vietnam, where he was outnumbered 4 to 1.

"A plan, like a tree, must have branches—if it is to bear fruit. A plan with a single aim is apt to prove a barren pole."—Basil Liddell Hart

"Success is just a matter of luck. Ask any failure.—Earl Wilson

"Do not be arrogant because of your knowledge."—From the hieroglyphic writings of the Egyptian Ptahhope (2400 BC). Some personal guidance quotes are timeless.

"At the end of our lives, I think it will be unlikely that we will be counting our money or cataloguing the toys we have accumulated. Instead, we are probably going to ask ourselves a question: Did I make a difference?—Chesley "Sully" Sullenberg, retired U. S. Airways pilot, from a commencement address at Purdue University.

"Public opinion is a weak tyrant compared with our own private opinion. What a man thinks of himself, that is it which determines his fate."—Henry David Thoreau

"Whatever the danger of the action we take, the dangers of inaction are far, far greater."—Tony Blair

"There is no passion to be found playing small—in settling for a life that's less than the one you're capable of living."—Nelson Man-dela

"Reading is a means of thinking with another person's mind; it forces you to stretch your own."—Charles Scribner, Jr.

"Unless you walk out into the unknown, the odds of making a profound difference in your life are pretty low."—Tom Peters

"Try, try, try. Keep trying, keep trying. Don't let the bastards get you (down)."—Meryl Streep

"Trust yourself. Create the kind of self that you will be happy to live with all your life. Make the most of yourself by fanning the tiny, inner sparks of possibility into flames of achievement."—Foster C. McClellan

"Life is a gift. Freedom is a responsibility."— Unknown

"I found that the men and women who got to the top were those who did the jobs they had in hand, with everything they had of energy and enthusiasm and hard work."—President Harry S. Truman

"If I had eight hours to chop down a tree, I'd spend six hours sharpening my ax."—Abraham Lincoln. In other words prepare thoroughly for the project at hand before beginning.

"We will either find a way, or make one."—Hannibal

"Destiny is not a matter of chance, it is a matter of choice; it is not a thing to be waited for, it is a thing to be achieved."—William Jennings Bryan

"The greater the difficulty the more glory in surmounting it. Skillful pilots gain their reputation from storms and tempests."—Epictetus

"Spare yourselves from the indulgence of self-pity. It is always self-defeating. Subdue the negative and emphasize the positive."—Gordon B. Hinckley

"Achievement seems to be connected with action. Successful men and women keep moving. They make mistakes, but they don't quit."—Conrad Hilton

"Life is not measured by the number of breaths you take, but with the number of moments that take your breath away."—Unknown

"Personal development is your springboard to personal excellence. Ongoing, continuous, non-stop personal development literally assures you that there is no limit to what you can accomplish."—Brian Tracy

"Courage is the first of human qualities because it is the quality that guarantees all the others."—Winston Churchill

"If a man hasn't discovered something he will die for, he isn't fit to live."—Martin Luther King Jr.

"If you believe you can, you probably can. If you believe you won't, you most assuredly won't. Belief is the ignition switch that gets you off the launching pad."—Dennis Waitley

"Attitude is more important than the past, than education, than money, than circumstances, than what people do or say. It is more important than appearance, giftedness, or skill."—Charles Swindoll

"The ripest peach is highest on the tree."—James Whitcomb Riley

"Without enthusiasm you are doomed to a life of mediocrity but with it you can accomplish miracles."—Og Mandino

"You lie the loudest when you lie to yourself."—Unknown

"First we form habits, then they form us. Conquer your bad habits or they will conquer you."—Rob Gilbert

"Dream what you want to dream—go where you want to go—try to be who you really are—because life is short and often gives us only a few chances to do the things that matter."—Unknown

"People with goals succeed because they know where they're going.—Earl Nightingale

"This one step—choosing a goal and sticking to it—changes everything."—Scott Reed

"You must have long term goals to keep you from being frustrated by short term failures."—Charles C. Noble

"Too many people are thinking of security instead of opportunity. They seem more afraid of life than death."—James F. Byrnes

"Take care of your body. It's the only place you have to live."—Jim Rohn

"Opportunity dances with those who are ready on the dance floor."—H. Jackson Brown Jr.

"Keep in mind that neither success nor failure is ever final."—Roger Ward Babson

"My motto was always to keep swinging. Whether I was in a slump or feeling badly or having trouble off the field, the only thing to do was keep swinging."—Hank Aaron

"Apply yourself. Get all the education you can, but then, by God, do something. Don't just stand there, make something happen."—Lee Iacocca

"People of mediocre ability sometimes achieve outstanding success because they don't know when to quit. Most men succeed because they are determined to."—George Allen

"One important key to success is self-confidence. An important key to self-confidence is preparation."—Arthur Ashe

"We are at our very best, and we are happiest, when we are fully engaged in work we enjoy on the journey toward the goal we've established for ourselves. It gives meaning to our time off and comfort to our sleep. It makes everything else in life so wonderful, so worthwhile."—Earl Nightingale

"If there is any one axiom that I have tried to live up to in trying to become successful in business, it is the fact that I have tried to surround myself with associates that know more about business than I do. This policy has always been very successful and is still working for me."—Monte L. Bean

"Always be loyal to those who are absent, if you want to retain those who are present."—Stephen Covey

"The kindest thing you can do for the people you care about is to become a happy, joyous person."—Brian Tracy

"Men give me credit for some genius. All the genius I have lies in this: When I have a subject in hand, I study it profoundly. Then the effort which I have made is what people are pleased to call the fruit of genius. It is the fruit of labor and thought."—Alexander Hamilton

"The great dividing line between success and failure can be expressed in five words: I did not have time."—Franklin Field

"If you get a second chance, grab it with both hands."—Unknown

"Pray as if everything depended on God and work as if everything depended on man."—Saint Augustine

"He who has health, has hope; and he who has hope, has every-thing."—Arabian Proverb

"I can't believe God put us on this earth to be ordinary."—Lou Holtz

"Live, so you do not have to look back and say: God, how I have wasted my life."-Elizabeth Kubler-Ross

"It is better to be vaguely right than precisely wrong."—John Maynard Keynes

"Life is too short to wake up with regrets. So love the people who treat you right."—Unknown

"If you lack the courage to start, you have already finished."—Unknown

"People who laugh actually live longer than those who don't laugh. Few persons realize that health actually varies according to the amount of laughter."—James Walsh

"The credit belongs to the man who is actually in the arena; whose face is marred by dust and sweat and blood; who strives valiantly; who errs and comes up short again and again; who knows the great enthusiasms, the great devotions, and spends himself in a worthy cause; who at the best knows in the end triumph of high achievement; and who at the worst, if he fails, at least he fails while daring greatly."—President Theodore Roosevelt

"Believe that life is worth living, and your belief will help create the fact."—William James

"Life is the ticket to the greatest show on earth."—Unknown

"I've learned that people will forget what you said, people will forget what you did, but people will never forget how you made them feel."—Unknown

"I never worry about action, but only inaction."—Winston Churchill

"Whenever you find yourself on the side of the majority, it is time to pause and reflect."—Mark Twain

"Grab 'em by the balls and their hearts and minds will soon follow."—Stanley Karnow

"Carpe diem." ("Seize the day." i.e. act now)—Horace

"I think I can. I think I can. I think I can."—Watty Piper, from her story *The Little Engine That Could.*

"I knew I could. I knew I could. I knew I could."—From the concluding page of the same story quoted above.

"I never in my life learned anything from a man who agreed with me."— Dudley Malone

"Success is falling down nine times and getting up ten."—Jon Bon Jovi

www.ingramcontent.com/pod-product-compliance
Lightning Source LLC
Chambersburg PA
CBHW031327040426
42443CB00005B/244